MY INKED TERRITORY

A POETRY COLLECTION

SUMEET MATHUR

ISBN 979-888606194-9

MY INKED TERRITORY:

A POETRY COLLECTION

BY SUMEET MATHUR

Contents

Contents

Preface

Enter the hour, enter the year, when what was bonnet becomes rear,
engulfed in a cloak of prospects new,
to bring in the courage and drive out fear!

Let's start the New Year 2019 with some verses! What say? Do you know who was 'Made' of Honor? Or what the orphan understood from the embers in the fireplace? How does it feel to pirouette into someone's arms? All the answers are hidden inside this poetry collection! Read on!

Acknowledgements

To the Lord Almighty, for everything.

To my father, Atul Mathur, who unwaveringly bears with all my unpredictability and supports all my endeavors to the last. Without him, life is just a dream.

To my mother Geeta Mathur and brother Akshay Mathur, who teach me every day what life actually means, even though they may find a sarcastic listener in me. They push me to give my best in everything.

To Rowling, Blyton and Tolkein (to name a few), for this insatiable excitement for the literary world.

To Frost, Shakespeare and the Music inside, for the poetic tendencies bubbling within.

And finally to all my family friends and acquaintances, for appreciating the author and poet in me and always encouraging me to pursue what I love. This book is testimony to that.

Last but not the least, to you, the reader for choosing to honor me with your precious time. I hope you enjoy the verses!

Table Of Contents

1. RESURRECTION 2019

Enter the hour, enter the year,
When what was bonnet becomes rear,
Engulfed in a cloak of prospects, new
to bring in the courage and drive out fear,
Courage to attempt, courage to succeed,
in every act and every deed,
when such courage is mustered well,
then why, Fear, for you is there need?
Fancy a Cake, fancy a drink?
Boy, health wise, we are all in the pink,
So some say, on the contrary, today
Let's thank to this health,
with work, duty and not with drink,
Awake the Angels in us all,
And Resolution after Resolution is made to stand tall,
some meaning it with all their heart,
and others, meaning it for the sake of it all,
Enough said,
Oaths, promises and dreams alike,
Bringing out of us, each determined spike,

This much we owe ourselves, Oh Yes,
The chance to boost ourselves and hike,
So we welcome this wonderful New Year,
with much warmth and humble cheer,
to give us happiness and peace aplenty,
in the times, both far and near.

---

2. THE ACES OF MANKIND

'Tis said more often than not,
And is truer than all other rot,
That in unity, lies our victory trot,
Caste, creed and color asunder,
For these splits are our biggest blunder,
Whether in sport or in nation,
From the simple to situation,
The meager and mighty, all are a part,
Thus, each will contribute with all their heart,
For,
Divided, we tend to lose all,
Otherwise, we get to stand tall,
Each opinion, each idea, each thought and each input,
Makes sure that we rarely venture a wrong foot,
And matter's not of the opinion giver,
Whether experienced or never clever,
For those at which are laughed upon,
In future, in them, Legends are born,
So,
In oneness must we dig our roots,

On Division should we hang our boots,
Giving ourselves the best chance,
To taste Success as the fruit of fruits,
If there were any superpowers in access,
they were always thus,
Faith, Unity, Cooperation and Success,
Sans them, the world blind,
Thus I call them,
The Aces of Mankind.

---

3. TEEN VERSERS

Oh! To be young and pull the strings,
Of life as how we please,
The strength to fathom, achieve and acquire,
Zeal blowing its lovely breeze,
With aid from friends, family and allies,
Impossible is nothing,
for as sharp as a collective force,
Nothing can sting,
But name and fame, there to win,
and equally to lose,
face your values and your work,
and you do get to choose,
The thrill, the speed,
and the fast world,
lure them away or let them lure,
in that your future, unfurled,
Always in vision is an easy way,
the way to succeed soon,
but if we select Easy over Right,
then how is Right a boon?
Young we be, spry and up,
But nevertheless yet young,

Respect, Follow and look up to the elder,
And victory bells can be rung,
Sure to be, fear the One,
Who gave us all we are,
Faith and Adherence can work wonders,
to succeed us, to farthest of far.

POEM 3
TEEN VERSERS

Oh! To be young and pull the strings,
Of life as how we please,
The strength to fathom, achieve and acquire,
Zeal blowing its lovely breeze,
With aid from friends, family and allies,
Impossible is nothing,
for as sharp as a collective force,
Nothing can sting,
But name and fame, there to win,
and equally to lose,
face your values and your work,
and you do get to choose,
The thrill, the speed,
and the fast world,
lure them away or let them lure,
in that your future, unfurled,
Always in vision is an easy way,
the way to succeed soon,

but if we select Easy over Right,
then how is Right a boon?
Young we be, spry and up,
But nevertheless yet young,
Respect, Follow and look up to the elder,
And victory bells can be rung,
Sure to be, fear the One,
Who gave us all we are,
Faith and Adherence can work wonders,
to succeed us, to farthest of far.

---

4. SERENDIPITY

Imagine what kind of a world would it be,
were all to be known before,
Everything we know that could happen, would happen,
And nothing were left in store,
The word surprise seems a rarity,
Where each of us make our joy,
some desperate, some deserving,
some in pain, oh boy!
Some events, special as ever,
Expected by all in yearn,
but the same if unexpected emerge,
Oh that would be what we'd rather earn!
For the glee in anything unforeseen,
Is glee to joy no bounds,
Meeting Somebody, achieving something,
or getting a thousand pounds,
Whether luck or fate cometh our side,
or our acts reap reward,
such happenstances be quite a welcome tide,
a tide by the Almighty Lord,
Stayeth forever in this manner,
our Providence or God's pity,

To grant us such, as welcome as ever,
Flashes of Serendipity.

---

5. ADVENTURE

Soft and sly, sudden and spry,
Joy for some and for some to cry,
Adventure scents the air around,
and life becomes a merry go round,
For some to seek and for some to stumble,
In pursuit or many a grumble,
Child, man or maiden alike,
The adrenaline sure gets the spike,
All of us with our own way,
To get adventure every day,
For some being life and soul,
Sans adventure each sulking ghoul,
For some it being hit and run,
For some it being random fun,
For some being passion and work,
For some even the thrill to shirk,
Whether it be a sport or an art,
The gleam of adventure shows right from the heart,
Passion, Perseverance and Sincerity for some,
Speak for their ventures and of success to come,
Hear! Our routine is not any less to complain,
for equal is the adventure of the mundane,

as is said, from times of yore,
Adventure begins when you step out the door,
So go on, live and love each adventure,
For the blood to pump and thrill to venture,
Let the excitement and happiness unfurl,
And the scent of adventure in this world, swirl!

---

6. CELESTIAL

As the dusk gives way for the clear night,
And one is taken up to the celestial bight,
A thought of a kind, starts to form,
The thought that to every human is a birthright norm,
One giant thought, for the giants above,
With levels of gas, say zillions of the stove,
These mighty orbs, it seemed, forever to last,
Twinkling and winking, at us, right from the past,
With naught to do but hang all day,
The interest they invoke, oh I say!
Sizes and shapes of all nature,
Fascinating to one and all, however mature!
The absence of sound, one would deem,
Only helps them stay within their seam,
For the noise of our planet is noise enough,
To last the universe of its steam,
Planets upon planets with moons upon moons!
Among astronomers and enthusiasts, causing varieties of swoons,
Such Wonderlands to discover and such knowledge to get,
Right from The Big Bang to the Haley's Comet!
Asteroid, quasar and black hole,
Capturing our imagination on the whole,

Oh why can't we just hop into one?
A spaceship that takes us to the Universe's soul!
The might of it all often strikes fear,
Of millions of miles and of each light year,
What spectacles to witness for belief to stand tall,
A creation to wonder at, for us all,
Oh to be celestial and wield such power!
And that thought on them always to hover,
Sure to be, hark! Space is a dream!
Always open to our fascination, it would seem!

---

7. FARE THEE WELL!

Sometimes I wonder
How life would have been,
Were childhood not for us
To have seen,
The tantrums, the naughtiness,
Loads to spare,
Beating our adults
Fair and square,
Ah, If anything we wish it,
This childhood swell,
We wish it with our hearts,
Fare Thee Well!
Sleep, hunger,
and fun alike,
Whether the clock
Would any hand strike,
Stories and lore,
what a joy to hear!
Whether it be family,
or anyone near!
Oh, If anything we wish it,
This childhood swell,

We wish it with our hearts,
Fare Thee Well!
Those lovely cartoon afternoons,
Fascinating as can be,
Among them, choosing our favorite,
Our hard task to be!
Who said we never did,
any of our homework?
Those notes we copied the next day in school,
Weren't they worthy of a Perk?
Ah well!
If anything we wish it,
This childhood swell,
We wish it with our hearts,
Fare Thee Well!
These years we live, in consolation,
Nay, half as joyous as Thee,
Happiness, Wealth and Age we muster,
But Childhood is a Spree!
If ever there was a Gift so worthy,
Be it doubtless your encore,
Oh! What would we not give to live that again,
Bliss as ever before!
Thus, we say,
If anything we wish it,
This childhood swell,
We wish it with our hearts,

Fare Thee Well!

---

8. HEED, O HALE!

Oh! Hearty and Hale!
Grant us a bail,
Why thou not give us a chance?
Tired of porridge and bread stale,
And of many a pitiable glance,
Oh! Hearty and Hale!
Drink to us ale,
that we be above this pittance,
Rid us soon of all that's frail,
with poverty facing the guns,
Oh! Hearty and Hale!
Lift up our scale,
we do have much to enhance,
Give us the learning, on that shall we sail,
Spill will we not any chance,
Oh! Hearty and Hale!
This you must hail,
Bring us into the peaceful trance,
Of us, the
Thinkers and doers, our service on sale,
From Italy to France,

Oh! Hearty and Hale!
Female and male,
each of us have a stance,
On politics, entertainment and every tale,
as rigid as a lance,
Oh! Hearty and Hale!
Like head and tail,
both sides, in us, to advance,
Nourish the good, for the bad to quail,
Get rid of all the askance,
Oh! Hearty and Hale!
Healers of every ail,
great are the cures in your hands,
Rid us all of all our ail,
And together, in bliss, shall we dance,
Oh! Hearty and Hale!
Do heed the pale,
Blow us some fragrance,
Change the odor, change our trail,
cast aside the avoidance,
Oh! Hearty and Hale!
Throw us the pail,
Of equality and hope in tons,
Get our children on the rail,
to education, where life runs,
Oh! Hearty and Hale!
On us, don't fail,

for, of same father, are we all sons,
The Merciful Lord of the Purest Vale,
Who's granted us all abundance,
So heed and give us unfounded ones,
the strength to stand on our own,
in this endeavor, if we succeed,
the might of humanity is shown.

---

9. INFINITY

One wonders how proud,
Infinity would be when,
the Infinite in the world,
think about Infinity,
to Infinity and beyond.
While Infinity reveals such,
As possibilities and discoveries anew,
Fantastic even,
For the Infinite in this land,
to ponder upon.
And thus I say,
Infinity intrigues,
The Infinite,
To Infinity and beyond!

---

10. PIROUETTE INTO MY ARMS

Drat that, what's a that,
a ceasing smile to be,
Why thou shalt account through it,
And Why for me to see?
For me to see shall be the crease that
perfectly fits your lips,
oh, flutter! When that happens,
My heart always trips!
Let not any worry or vice get through to you that harms,
Lighten, smile your worries at me,
And Pirouette into my Arms.
Take my word, our biggest worry is how to not get worried,
But challenge or Fate, whichever it is, to worry, into are we hurried,
But each other we have forever,
to share and care always,
Let not the medicine that I get from your smile, from me part ways,

That dimple of yours, open it up, the one that always charms,
just enter the World that we made for ourselves,
And Pirouette into my Arms.
What I see in us that matters,
others will see it not,
For Perfection is not something that all can see,
It's a gift from Above in a lot,
For you to see too
is this blissful feeling present,
If you could not and what a shame!
Then why is it Special, the moon crescent?
So endure, ignore and ensure,
that shake you not the worldly norms,
Justice to your silhouette do,
and gently Pirouette into My Arms.
Hath not seen a prettier sight,
than your happiness blooming before,
How can there be a problem for me,
without you as my certain cure?
Heed, O world! Stand your guard,
for hassle us you cannot,
nothing stands in the power of love,
And anybody dare not!
With me as your heart for life,
Your journey will be green as the farms,
As long as we live, throw aside all else,
And Pirouette into My Arms.

---

11. THE INFLAMED ORPHAN

Amidst the embers, emerged the men,
Dancing, smiling and waving,
As flames engulfed their silhouettes,
As well as danced in her eyes,
She, an orphan, in memory of them,
them, her parents, in Heaven,
for flames it was that consumed them,
having visited a year back,
This little girl, devastated, took too much to flames,
And sat by the fireplace every night,
Waiting for their faces;
To appear, comfort and love her.
Then it was that had emerged,
As dancing men, in flames,
Friendship the least they offered,
Heeding the tale of this orphan,
They made to be her only attraction,
For they were in flames.
Asked She to them a day,
How doth thou exist?

The dancing men beam and utter such;
"Thy parents knew thee best,
Thus we exist."
So saying the dancing men made way for two faces,
Faces long desired by her,
Faces that inspire her to make them proud,
And not seclude,
"The creator, He sends us to you,
to prove He is always with you"
They smiled and the girl, she smiled back for;
She felt God.

---

12. MADE OF HONOR

Her eyes flashed me,
The same look that always took me by joy,
Every time,
As when she got her favorite comb,
Or when she passed any test, oh Boy!
Standing there in her wedding dress,
Upon the brink of her second innings of life,
Finally sufficing me that,
She could also be tall, the reason for many our strife!
As the memories of my bullying her flowed in,
And our Goldilocks Height scale concurred,
I felt an impression,
An impression of affection that made merry between us,
One that long ago stirred,
That now beheld a stunning bride,
A lovely wife to be,
And in that bride,
I saw my best ever friend,
And like a sister to me,
These hands of mine would guide Her soon,
Soon to the marriage aisle,
Like puddles I used to help Her cross before,

Only, here it was more joy and hale!
What started out as a huge crush,
One that stayed long in my ear,
And here we were in their union,
As I blinded back a happy tear,
Although best friends, we were for sure,
but not her only ones,
for me such an Honor to uphold,
her faith proved in abundance,
Overpowering Prospects of fear and failure,
engulfing me whole,
but that impression of affection,
It adequately my heart, stole.
Tomorrow come, this beautiful bride will step into a new sunrise,
with a friend, a sister and partner for every shock and surprise,
Of her life, for her will I always play every genre,
as now, has crossed my Fate,
to be her Maid of Honor,
With much thought I say that this is what I think,
forgive me if in the face of Philosophy I blink,
But Maid of Honor indeed can be each, one and all,
but to be 'Made' of Honor in soul is what it takes to stand tall.

---

13. THE ABOMINABLE SNOWMAN

Ere the snow that starts to fall,
the paths are cleared for feet to stroll,
Feet of a Being one man too many,
Humongous from without, but within as honey,
Many a mountaineer peered upon,
From the dims of dusk to the daze of dawn,
To solve this puzzle would He give His penny,
As to why these people cometh here so many?
Some wearing animal fur,
While some wearing frowns on their spur,
Some for passing out on the tracks,
While some for waving their country's flags,
Why oh why, do they run as much,
As when He comes in their sight,
Do they not see the harmlessness,
Hiding behind all His might?
These humans, what a life they lead!
Amidst noise, pollution and creed,
Oh! Ask them to pitch their tents over here,
where one can drool over the beauty of our sphere!

Snowed mountains as white as pure,
The Horizon even admiring, for sure!
With flawless rise and towering peaks,
enough to addle the brains of the geeks!
So saying, our Abominable Snowman,
Casts a grimace at the newest caravan,
it's time to scare and deceive from without,
for that's the only activity He is able to sprout,
These lands of snow, till when they last,
The Abominable Snowmen will hold to them fast,
For times immemorial have they, their gazes cast,
And will have to now, even more than the past.
So free your breath and don't get sweaty,
It's just The Adorable Mountain Yeti,
One almost as human as us,
With God's Grace, even more cleverer than us!

---

14. THE HYDRA QUEEN

"Ahoy there, set sail!"
Came the Captain's voice,
Masts high and timber gleaming,
Showing off its sailing poise,
"The Hydra Queen" it shone
with magnificence and pride,
Alas! This day had come,
for this vessel's much awaited ride,
The buzz increased
as well as should, every eye wide,
as steam escaped the royal vessel,
the ship taking its stride,
On the deck stood the children,
Taking it all in,
And seeing their wonder and their joy,
The sailors each afforded a grin,
To port side; all eyes turned,
As the seagulls made their presence felt,
Gliding around the masts, and rising,
As beauty in front of them, knelt,

Lo! Realized every person,
Water was land for them,
Engulfed breathtakingly on all the sides,
at its mercy to hem,
At the distance, was a sight,
All would crave to see,
The Horizon where the sun and water met,
Why! Was it like that to be free!
Behold! Blew in the west winds,
The might of it surreal,
Bringing with it tales of far and old,
Filled with both sadness and zeal,
Screams of delight ranked the air,
as starboard brimmed with life,
Schools of dolphins, tempting the vessel;
Oh excitement on this day was rife!
Thereupon settled in the eventful dusk,
as enthusiastic as ever,
Dances, games, dinner on deck,
why, joy today was a fever!
Observing all this, on the platform,
The Captain gave a nod,
this first Sail of The Queen,
Was worthy of applaud,
Such journeys and such times
for us to get and cheer,
May we relish all this beauty,

in the times, distant and near!

---

15. THE LAST PROCESSION

That powerful voice which commanded all,
whether it be summer or autumn fall,
Ninety years lived our mighty King,
Alas! It's time for us now, a lament to sing,
A lament fitting this last procession,
One that would match His unfaltering precision,
Thousands of us saddened, walk this way,
As tomorrow dawns a King-less day,
Hearts heavy, as tears shed,
For such a King, for whom love spread,
One and all, in the procession,
moved by his every action and decision,
Ah! There was a time when royalty traipsed,
Traipsed magnificently along to kingdoms and war,
But today all that is erased,
This royalty will reach only the pyre thus far,
A pyre worthy of cities myriad,
In which the King will rest, honorably clad,
Each heart praying aloud,
That rest not with him, may the justness he had,

Why oh why, such irony do we see?
Where once was a King is a memory-to-be,
Wielding swords and ruling a time,
And in a pyre come years to chime!
Such is the mystery of life, for sure!
To reap, our own doings will endure,
Be it a pauper or a mighty King,
Each will face this formidable thing,
Thus, ends the final stroll,
Of a mighty King of the Royal Hall,
One whose rule was a noble session,
As is evident from this Last Procession!

---

16. YOURS FAITHFULLY

Two lanes, emerge into sight,
One of cheek and the other of might,
The left, easy and comfy,
towards a goal too sweet,
While the right, for all its roughness,
Offering just the perfect meat,
Whilst I ponder the options,
Two voices bellow within,
The clash of both voices enraging,
My choice grows thin,
Cackling, menacing and what-not,
one of the voices attract,
but honesty and purity shown,
the other seems the hero of the act,
"Take the left, succeed fast!"
Screams the Attractive voice,
"Right yourself, cherish your past"
Whispers our Heroic voice,
This grass path, sneers Attractive,
"Green and soft for you!"

But for all the praise for that path,
there is no softness in his voice, that's true!
Heroic's demeanor reassuring,
My eyes turn towards the right,
And through the raging snarls of Attractive,
I know I have corrected my sight,
Thus, smiling to myself,
The right path I start to tread,
A path ridding me of many things,
Some being impatience and greed,
Defeated left the Attractive voice,
The Devil inspiring folly,
Beaming embraced me, my Heroic Conscience,
Signing- Yours Faithfully.

---

17. THE MERRY LOT

Oh! Light the fires and pitch the tents,
Cook the soup and count the cents,
Merrily, Merrily, you shall see,
What we stand for, from ages whence!
Eat the sword, and juggle fine!
Walk the rope and climb the vine,
Merrily, Merrily, you shall live,
what we have, on our own timeline!
Tame a lion or a caravan,
Sing for yourself or for the clan,
Merrily, Merrily, you shall smile,
And help yourself to our span!
Trick with a card or cart your wheel,
But do what you may, with all your zeal,
Merrily, Merrily, you shall learn,
That who we are and how we feel,
Awaken the mirth or laugh yourself,
Wag your ears and be like an elf,
Merrily Merrily, you shall get,
The comics' secrets off the shelf,
Whether it be a Hall or barn,
Of happiness, do we always weave the yarn,

Merrily, Merrily, you shall jump,
At how we entertain, oh Darn!
The joy on the faces of people, to see,
Brings more into us, than them, the glee,
Oh, Merrily Merrily, you shall glide,
In our joyous entertaining spree,
Now! Follow the Guv'nor and help the Gran,
to learn and eat all you can,
Merrily Merrily, you shall be,
A part of this boisterous caravan!
Right! Should the need arise,
Or if there is any entertainment for us, to prize,
Well, in the countryside or beyond the oak,
Next to the streams, or at any fork,
Merrily, Merrily, you shall find,
Us Proud Circus-Folk!

---

18. US HENCHMEN

There are some of us for sure,
Who would prefer to follow rather than lure,
Whether or not a justified stance,
With our leader, we would take no chance,
Us Henchmen, strong and proud,
Following our leader from induction to the shroud,
Some who question our very need,
To answer this question, we humbly plead,
That if each would become a leader in need,
Who would we look towards to carry out the deed?
Some are created to set examples,
While some to follow and yet be samples,
Whether by protection or implementation,
In our loyalty would occur only inflation,
We are here to glorify our leader's reign,
Whether it makes it easy or gives us pain,
So saying, we bow in submission,
As we are granted our next mission,
In the hope to give it our best,
And pass our life's premium test!

19. OUR SKILLED LADY

These verses we penned down today,
Are right from our heart,
For you whom we have much to thank for,
Oh right from the start!
You, our skills teacher, as fitting as could be,
One who could mould us in life, though busy as a bee,
Life of mundane, you did avert,
Leading to your destiny,
Spreading happiness and confidence unbound,
Causing a mutiny,
A mutiny between us and our minds,
Which needed a person like you,
Clear, strong and positive,
Respectful of all virtue,
These days we spent in harmony,
Gazed have we on your ways,
Of the perfectionist and the spry one inside,
Desired have we to reflect that gaze,
The Skill Class as they would call it,
Just opened our thinking to heights,

Each of us wondering to ourselves,
Have we found the lights?
Most of all, we admire how
You got all of us to gel,
Forcing us to vent always,
That ring not may the bell!
May you have all the happiness, our skilled lady,
For now, we must make you smile,
And get that frown shady,
So saying, we bid you,
The most hearty farewell,
With loads of gratitude overflowing in us,
May you get everything swell!

---

20. SCIENCE

The discovery of Science,
Has led to finds,
That have fascinated minds,
And led to all kinds,
Of paralleled lines.
That line each defines,
From its confines,
Of many a possibility that shines,
To remove some blinds,
Around the secrets of Science!
Having drawn many blinds,
Right from tools to strange mines,
Bringing humans from helpless hinds,
To the foremost of master minds!
This knowledge that entwines,
And fascinates us despite its grinds,
Becomes the source that always for us winds,
One that sustains us; our very own Science.

---

21. SEP'MEMBER'

Today, along the college chamber,
Do we pray for a special gang member,
One whom anyone would befriend indeed,
Who always gives her best in every deed and need,
For today, Her day of birth turns up,
And everything that's Black goes proudly heads up,
The smile on her face, Oh worthy of a sketch,
She could do it herself, it is her passion to fetch!
But confined to sketching is not her expertise,
For with her studies,
all of us does she tease,
Her performance, impressive and worthy of applaud,
Making her a competitor,
Of a very strong chord,
When it comes to organizing,
She must be the queen,
For everything is systematic,
That can be seen,
Oh and if there were anything to be designed,
All it would take is to capture her mind,
For that always seems to be her cup of tea,
A healthy drop of water in a fashion sea,

So saying, we pray for our lovely friend,
That the best of the years greet her,
Our own gang member turns nineteen,
This lovely September,
With all our love and affection, do we wish her today,
The most of happiness for her life and a very happy birthday!

---

22. SWEET AND SOUR!

When the going gets tough,
And Success seems bleak,
Some Hope is bound to be,
A Hope that kindles traces of success,
Oh! What a Sweet to me!
A Sweet that may be very well earned,
Or simply a respite from God,
Whichever it is, used rightly must it be,
Lest it behave'th like a fraud,
But as always, there will be opposites,
As a stinking side to the flower,
Where Sweetness is in excess or isn't in access,
There will be the imminent Sour,
Spoiling the party for many a joy,
When the wheels are in motion,
Just when our efforts start bearing fruit,
Sour acts as the nasty potion,
Trust your effort, but never your success,
For Sour will always linger,
Endurance and Will are the weapons,
To subdue its ill-willed anger,

Sweet and Sour, both sides of our coin,
Sent to balance our equation,
One will heal, if the other will not,
This Faith one must hold in ration,
In full effort lies our key to all,
Whether the task easy or tough,
So believe that,
For Sweet to overtake Sour for us,
That might just be enough!

---

23. ADIEU

Now we come to the pages last few,
Where I bid you all Adieu,
Verse and Prose and line and letter,
Hope this book has made you feel better,
If the Pensieve you liked, then this Territory you may have loved,
Or if not, both books you may have shoved,
If it is prose and not poetry you seek,
In that also soon shall I give you a peek!
In this book,
Amongst the lines I made to rhyme,
A message was hidden all the time,
Waiting for your eyes to pierce it's meaning,
Did we all enhance our learning?
At times, there may have been a blunder,
Please don't on my faults, you plunder!
For mighty are those who do forgive,
I did have at least good poetry to give!
Till next time, when I return with more,
And deliver good words that should work like cure,
I sign off with all thanks to you,
And bid you the best 'Adieu'!

Printed by Libri Plureos GmbH in Hamburg,
Germany